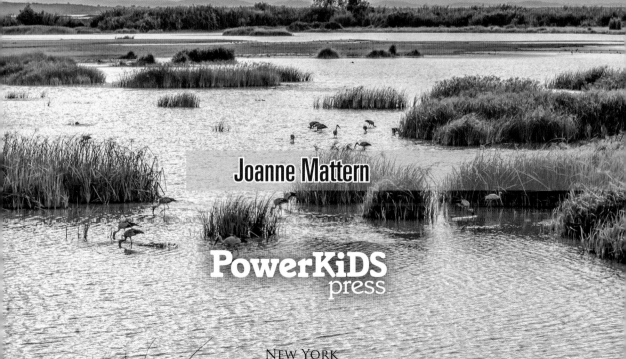

How Do You Live There?

LIVING IN SWAMPS, SALT MARSHES, AND OTHER WETLANDS

Joanne Mattern

PowerKiDS press

NEW YORK

Published in 2021 by The Rosen Publishing Group, Inc.
29 East 21st Street, New York, NY 10010

Editor: Kristen Susienka
Designer: Rachel Rising

Photo Credits: Cover, Mongkolchon Akesin/Shutterstock.com; Cover, pp.3,4,6,8,9,10,11,12,14,16,18,19,20,21,22, 23,24,25,26,27,28,30,31(background) Yevhenii Borshosh/Shutterstock.com; pp. 4, 5 MarcelClemens/Shutterstock. com; p. 7 Kanokratnok/Shutterstock.com; p. 9 Jason Dozark/Shutterstock.com; p. 10 ivSky/Shutterstock.com; p. 11 higrace/Shutterstock.com; p. 13 Bettmann/Contributor/Getty Images; p. 15 areporter/Shutterstock.com; p. 17 Songquan Deng/Shutterstock.com; p.19 Tim Roberts Photography/Shutterstock.com; p. 20 oneinchpunch/ Shutterstock.com; p. 21 CLP Media/Shutterstock.com; p. 23 Zharate/Shutterstock.com; p. 25 Jillian Cain Photography/ Shutterstock.com; p. 26 RichHiggins/Shutterstock.com; p. 27 J.D.S/Shutterstock.com; p. 28 Dennis W Donohue/ Shutterstock.com; p. 29 Vadim Petrakov/Shutterstock.com; p. 30 aaltair/Shutterstock.com.

Cataloging-in-Publication Data

Names: Mattern, Joanne.
Title: Living in swamps, salt marshes, and other wetlands / Joanne Mattern.
Description: New York : PowerKids Press, 2021. | Series: How do you live there? | Includes glossary and index.
Identifiers: ISBN 9781725316591 (pbk.) | ISBN 9781725316614 (library bound) | ISBN 9781725316607 (6 pack)
Subjects: LCSH: Wetlands--Juvenile literature. | Wetland ecology--Juvenile literature. | Swamps--Juvenile literature. | Swamp ecology--Juvenile literature. | Marshes--Juvenile literature. | Marsh ecology--Juvenile literature.
Classification: LCC QH541.5.M3 M28 2021 | DDC 577.68--dc23

Manufactured in the United States of America

Some of the images in this book illustrate individuals who are models. The depictions do not imply actual situations or events.

CPSIA Compliance Information: Batch #CSPK20. For further information contact Rosen Publishing, New York, New York at 1-800-237-9932.

Find us on

CONTENTS

WET PLACES

Earth has some very wet places. In fact, water makes up about 70 percent of Earth's surface. Lots of this water is in the oceans. Some, however, is in bodies of water on land, such as rivers, streams, or lakes.

Some of the wettest places on land are wetlands. A wetland is a place where the ground holds a lot of water. The water can come from flooding. Sometimes the water seeps, or slowly comes up, out of the ground. Other times, the water runs off from streams and rivers and gathers in an area on land. Swamps and salt marshes are two of the many types of wetlands.

Life in these wet places can be hard. However, many people and animals call wetland areas home. The plants in wetland areas have also **adapted** to living in soggy soil.

Other Important Wetlands

Salt marshes and swamps are only two types of wetlands. Other types include lagoons, deltas, mangroves, and **bayous**. A lagoon is a shallow, salty body of water surrounded by banks of sand. A delta is a watery area at the end of a river. A mangrove is a large coastal area where tall mangrove trees grow. A bayou is a slow-moving, swampy part of a river or lake.

Earth is full of water, but only a small part of that water is on land.

MARSHES AND SWAMPS

Swamps and salt marshes are on every continent except Antarctica. That's because Antarctica is frozen!

A marsh is almost always filled with water. Marshes aren't as deep as lakes, rivers, or the ocean. You can tell the difference between a marsh and a lake because marsh water is lower, and tall grasses usually grow in marshes. Lily pads, cattails, and reeds also grow there.

There are two types of marsh. Some marshes are saltwater marshes. These are usually near the coast, where ocean water fills the marshes. Other marshes are freshwater marshes. These are usually found along the shores of lakes, ponds, or rivers.

Unlike marshes, which have mostly grasses, swamps are home to trees and shrubs. Swamps often have deeper water than marshes, but not always. Like marshes, swamps can have salty or fresh water.

The Pantanal is the largest wetland in the world. Depending on the season, it can cover as much as 81,000 square miles (210,000 square kilometers) in Brazil, Bolivia, and Paraguay. That's about half the size of California!

WILDLIFE IN WETLANDS

Many different animals live in swamps, salt marshes, and other wetlands. The water holds fish, frogs, and insects. Large reptiles such as alligators and crocodiles love these wet habitats. So do snakes, crabs, and other **burrowing** creatures. Wetlands are also home to many different kinds of birds. Red-tailed hawks fly through the sky. Herons and egrets perch near the water. Woodpeckers find homes in the trees. These birds have plenty of fish, insects, and plants to eat. All of these creatures live near or in the wetland waters.

Mammals love wetlands too. Beavers build homes in wet places. Capybaras and muskrats live near the water as well. Large wetland predators include black bears and cougars.

Wetlands have also become places where people live, work, and play. They have built **sturdy** houses. Many use technology to help them live safely and comfortably.

The Florida Everglades

The Everglades is a large marsh in Florida. It covers more than 2.75 million acres (1.1 million hectares). A thick, tough plant called sawgrass grows there. Many different animals live in the Everglades, including panthers, herons, alligators, and crocodiles. Some people live in houses near the Everglades. They travel by special boats called airboats.

GREAT BLUE HERON

Wetlands are places where many birds make their homes.

DANGEROUS WETLANDS

Wetlands are not easy places to live. All that water can make life difficult in many different ways. There are many dangers in swamps, salt marshes, and other wetlands. The soggy ground can make it hard to walk. A person might trip over something they can't see under the water. Or they could get stuck in mud or lose their way in the thick **vegetation**.

Dangerous animals live in these areas too. Alligators, crocodiles, and poisonous snakes are all found in wetlands. Wetlands are also home to many mosquitoes, which spread deadly diseases.

Those who live in wetlands have to be careful. However, people have lived in wet environments for thousands of years. For the people who live there, wetlands provide food, protection, and housing.

MOSQUITOES

The Panama Canal

Swampy land was a big problem when workers built the **Panama Canal** in the early 1900s to connect the Atlantic and Pacific Oceans. Thousands of workers died from mosquito-spread diseases, such as yellow fever and malaria. However, mosquitoes were just one danger there. Workers had to cut through thick vegetation. They worked in hot, **humid** weather with lots of rain. They also faced death from mudslides and flooding.

People have to be careful when they visit wetlands. The ground is soggy, and there are insects that can bite and annoy.

WETLAND LIVING LONG AGO

People have called wetland areas home for hundreds of years. One ancient wetland group was the Maya. The Maya lived in Central America more than 1,000 years ago. Scientists used to think that the Maya only lived in cleared forest. However, they now believe that many of these ancient people lived and worked in swamps. They built canals and raised fields above the water in order to grow crops, or plants grown for use as food. These crops included corn, squash, and beans. Communities of up to 2,000 people were able to live in the swamps.

People have also used wetlands as places to hide and stay safe. When slavery was practiced in the United States, **fugitive slaves** often hid in southern swamps. It was difficult for others to find them in the thick trees and wet ground.

Before slavery ended in 1865, many African American slaves hid in swamps or marshes when they ran away from their owners. ├────────────────────────►

In the 1600s, the Great Dismal Swamp covered lots of land in southeastern Virginia and northeastern North Carolina. It had thick forests, lots of mud, and islands. Back then, Native American tribes that lived in the area used the swamp islands to hide from European explorers who were settling in their homeland. It was impossible for horses or large boats to get through the swamp's wet ground and thick trees. That made it a great hiding place.

Native Americans built communities in the swamp. Later, escaped slaves and white people hiding from the law also took **refuge** there. Although the swamp was a brief hiding place for most, some people chose to raise families there. Today, much of the swamp has been drained of water. Still, large parts of it are a wildlife park, which protects all the plants and animals that live there.

Many Native Americans who lived in swampy areas used boats called pirogues to travel through the water. They had flat bottoms and were lower to the water than other boats. ⊢——————➤

DRAINING THE WETLANDS

For many years, people thought wetlands were something to get rid of. They were dangerous and took up space, without providing clear benefits. People couldn't farm or build houses on the wetlands' soggy soil. For these reasons, people and governments around the world drained many wetland areas.

Draining an area gets rid of the water there. This can be done by digging canals to move the water elsewhere or by piling up dirt on top of the wetland to create dry land. Without so much water, people can start farms and build houses, businesses, and roads. Entire cities have been built on drained wetlands. Washington, D.C., and Fort Lauderdale, Florida, are two examples.

Today, about half of the wetlands in the United States have been drained. However, the United States has not been the only country to do this. Wetlands have been drained in other countries as well.

Washington, D.C., was a swamp that was drained to make the capital city.

SAVING THE WETLANDS

Over time, people realized that draining wetlands was causing all sorts of problems. Wetlands are a major way to control flooding. Water stored in swamps and marshes keeps the streets and homes of communities nearby safe from floods. With fewer wetlands, lots of flooding was happening.

Destroying wetlands also destroys habitats. Getting rid of mosquitoes that live in the wetlands might be a good thing to some, but draining a wetland also means taking away the homes of all the other creatures that live there. As more wetlands were destroyed, millions of birds, reptiles, mammals, and fish were left homeless. Some died.

In the early 1970s, scientists and governments realized that draining wetlands was a mistake. They began to restore them. These efforts helped reduce flooding. They also provided clean water and new habitats for animals and plants.

Tres Rios

In the 1990s, the city of Phoenix, Arizona, worked with the U.S. government to create the Tres Rios Demonstration Project. Tres Rios used wastewater plus water from streams and rivers to create a new wetland. Today, the area is filled with birds and other animals. The new wetland also **filters** out deadly materials and cleans the water.

Today, no vehicles are allowed to enter Tres Rios. However, people can enjoy hiking, birdwatching, horseback riding, and fishing there.

FUN IN THE WETLANDS

Today, many wetlands are recreation areas, or places where people can enjoy the outdoors. People come to swamps and marshes to enjoy sports such as fishing and hunting. Others can hike or go boating. Still more come to bird-watch. Wetlands are home to hundreds of **species** of birds.

Millions of people visit national parks in the United States and other countries every year. Many of these parks include wetlands. Some may be small, while others are quite large. Some national parks are made entirely of wetlands. Everglades National Park in Florida is one example.

EVERGLADES, FLORIDA

Narrow waterways lined with thick vegetation wind through the Okefenokee Swamp in Georgia.

OKEFENOKEE, GEORGIA

Other areas, like the Okefenokee Swamp in Georgia, are national wildlife refuges. People visit these parks to hike, fish, and see the many animals and plants that live there. Modern **vehicles** such as airboats make it easier to travel through the waterways.

In addition to being places to have fun, some wetlands are places to work. Louisiana is home to many bayous near the Mississippi River. These slow-moving waters are filled with shrimp, crawfish, catfish, and other types of sea life. Many factories have been built in the area to farm, catch, and process these creatures for food. In fact, more than 75 percent of the United States' **commercial** seafood comes from wetlands.

Wetland plant life can be another source of jobs. Wild rice grows naturally in the lakes and marshes of Minnesota. Traditionally, Native American groups like the Ojibwa traveled these northern waters in canoes, gathering the wild rice. Today, many people earn money by harvesting the rice in the same way. Others have flooded fields to create their own wetlands, called paddies, where they can grow the rice and harvest it with machines.

Protected Lands

Many wetlands are protected. That means they can't be built on. If a person wants to build a structure in a wetland, he or she needs special permission. The U.S. government wants to make sure that the wildlife and the habitat won't be in danger.

One of the best places in the United States to find wild rice is in the wetlands of Minnesota.

TODAY'S WETLAND LIFE

Today, communities built in wetlands are growing. Cities like Washington, D.C., and Fort Lauderdale continue to be popular places to live. Some wetlands are still being drained of their water. However, wildlife habitats are always thought about before wetlands are built on, and large areas of wetlands are being protected. Even though draining areas dries out the land and makes it easier to build houses or businesses, problems still arise. For example, buildings face damage from water if the community floods.

Still, many people enjoy living in or near wetlands. Residents, or people who live in an area, enjoy the outdoors. Boating, fishing, and hunting are popular sports. Swamps and marshes may be wet and humid, but they are also beautiful places to live. People who live there enjoy being close to nature and wildlife. They share community events and form close ties.

Food of the Wetlands

Food plays an important role in many wetland communities. Two major groups in Louisiana's wetland areas are the Cajuns and the Creoles. Cajuns have a French background, while Creoles have a mix of French, Spanish, Native American, and African roots. Both groups enjoy local seafood and bold flavors.

Many people like the wetlands around Fort Lauderdale, Florida, for the sunshine and activities there.

CLIMATE CHANGE

Today, more communities are trying to protect the areas where they live. They are also using wetlands to help stop dangers the planet faces.

One danger is climate change. Climate change is the shift in weather patterns over time due to lots of harmful gases crowding the air. The gases come from factory, car, and airplane fumes. Climate change is harming Earth and all life on it. However, wetlands may be our planet's best protection against it.

Blakemere Moss is a wetland in Delamere Forest, England. Hotter than usual summer weather caused the water level to drop, revealing the stumps of old trees.

Wetlands can help battle climate change.

Warmer temperatures from climate change cause more coastal flooding. Wetlands are **barriers** against flooding. Water collects there. Salt marshes can absorb, or take in, extra water instead of letting it flood coastal communities. Wetland plants like mangrove trees absorb **carbon dioxide** from the air and put oxygen into the air. This keeps the temperature from rising too much.

A PLACE FOR WETLANDS

Wetlands are very special places. Whether it is a coastal salt marsh or a swamp along a river, these places make our planet a better—and wetter—place. Without them, animals would be without homes, the air would be more polluted, and there would be fewer places for people to boat, fish, and enjoy nature.

It's important to remember wetlands when you think of habitats around the world. They have many different plants and animals living in them. Because of this, people must work together to protect them. When you're thinking about wetlands, ask yourself these questions: How do wetlands protect animals and plants that live there? Why should people keep them safe? What things can you do to help the wetlands?

ALLIGATOR

Wetlands are special places that should be protected and enjoyed.

WETLANDS AROUND THE WORLD

WETLAND	WHAT IS IT	LOCATION
Sundarbans	Saltwater swamp and mangrove forest	Bangladesh and India
Mareeba Tropical Savanna and Wetland Reserve	A variety of swamp, marsh, and lagoons	Australia
Danube Delta	Wetlands connecting the Danube River with the Black Sea	Ukraine, Romania, and Moldova
Okefenokee National Wildlife Refuge	Swamp	Georgia, U.S.A.
Pantanal Wetlands	Largest wetlands on Earth	Brazil, Bolivia, and Paraguay
Okavango	Large inland freshwater marsh	Botswana

DANUBE DELTA

GLOSSARY

adapt: To adjust to new conditions.

barrier: An object, such as a fence, that stops things from passing through it.

bayou: A very slow-moving body of water that resembles a marsh.

burrow: To dig and live underground.

carbon dioxide: A gas released into the air when coal, oil, and other fuels are burned.

commercial: Describing something that is bought or sold.

filter: To remove dirt or other unwanted elements from something.

fugitive slave: A person living between the 1600s and 1800s, owned by another person, who ran from their life to find freedom elsewhere.

humid: Having a high level of water in the air.

Panama Canal: A channel of water, made by humans, that connects the Atlantic and Pacific Oceans.

refuge: A place of shelter and safety.

species: A single type of plant or animal.

sturdy: Strong and able to withstand powerful winds or weather.

vegetation: Another name for plants, shrubs, or grasses growing in one place.

vehicle: A car, truck, boat, or other machine for traveling from place to place.

INDEX